# The Nature Kid's Guide to
# TAPIRS

## DAVID ANDERSON

LP Media Inc. Publishing
Text copyright © 2026 by LP Media Inc.
All rights reserved.



For information address LP Media Inc. Publishing,
30012 Variolite St NW, Princeton MN 55371
www.lpmedia.org

Publication Data

Tapirs
The Nature Kid's Guide to Tapirs — First edition.

Summary: "Learn all about Tapirs, the Nature Kid Way"
— Provided by publisher.

ISBN: 979-8-89818-257-1

[1. Tapirs – Non-Fiction] I. Title.

Title: The Nature Kid's Guide to Tapirs

# CONTENTS

# PECULIAR PARTS

**Crunch! A strange looking animal munches on leaves deep in the jungle.**

A tapir looks like no other animal. It has a round body, short legs, and a long, bendy nose. People say it looks part pig, part hippo!

Tapirs are heavy. A grown one can weigh up to 800 pounds. That is more than four grown people put together!

Surprisingly, the tapir is a close cousin of horses and rhinos. They do not look alike at all. But scientists know all three belong in the same animal group!

FUNKY TRUNKS
FUN FACT!
A tapir can use its trunk as a snorkel, breathing air while its body hides underwater!

**Sniff! A tapir's wiggly nose stretches out to grab a juicy berry.**

A tapir's nose is its best tool. The top lip and nose join to make a short **trunk**. This trunk can bend and twist just like a finger.

Tapirs use their trunk to pull leaves and fruit off branches. It helps them reach food that other animals miss. The trunk has thousands of muscles, making it super strong and flexible.

A tapir also sniffs with its trunk. It can smell friends and enemies from far away. That wiggly nose works hard all day and night!

# FOUR TYPES

The mountain tapir grows such a thick woolly coat it can survive temperatures that would freeze most tropical animals!
FUN FACT!

**Huff! A woolly mountain tapir picks its way through the cold Andean fog high above the clouds.**

There are four kinds of tapirs alive today, and they could not look more different from each other.

The South American tapir wades through steamy Amazon rainforests. Baird's tapir roams the thick jungles of Central America. The Malayan tapir — the only one found in Asia — wears a dramatic black and white coat that makes it look like a panda crossed with a pig.

The mountain tapir lives high in the freezing Andes Mountains, bundled in a thick woolly coat. No other tapir comes close to that.

# BUILT TOUGH

Tapirs take long mud baths to cool down and coat their skin against pesky bugs!

## Crash! A tapir barrels through a wall of thick jungle vines.

Tapirs are built to push through the thick rainforest. Their round, heavy bodies work like bulldozers. They crash through vines and thick brush with ease.

Tough, thick skin covers a tapir from head to tail. This armor can be almost an inch thick on the neck! It keeps thorns and sharp branches from hurting them. Even bug bites have a hard time getting through.

Tapirs have wide feet that keep them from sinking in mud. Strong legs carry them over steep hills. Every part of a tapir is made for life in the jungle.

# BABY SPOTS

FUN FACT!
A mother tapir has only one baby at a time and stays pregnant for 13 months!

**Squeak! A tiny baby tapir with spots and stripes peeks out.**

Baby tapirs are born with white stripes and spots. The pattern looks just like a watermelon! The light marks stand out on their dark brown fur.

These stripes help a baby hide in the forest. The spots blend in with the shadows on the ground. A predator may walk right past and miss it completely!

As the baby grows, the marks start to fade. By about six months old, they are gone. The young tapir then looks just like its parents, ready to face the world.

# BLACK AND WHITE

**Whoosh! A black and white tapir slips through the trees.**

The Malayan tapir lives in the forests of Southeast Asia. It is the only tapir outside the Americas. It is also the biggest of all four kinds, weighing up to 1,100 pounds!

This tapir has a bold look. Its head and legs are jet black. A big white patch covers the middle of its body like a saddle.

That pattern helps it hide at night. In the dark, the white patch breaks up its shape. A hungry hunter sees a blob, not a tapir!

# BIG BAIRD'S

DID YOU KNOW?
A mother Baird's tapir stays with her calf for up to two years, teaching it forest secrets!

**Thud! A huge Baird's tapir stomps along a muddy riverbank.**

Baird's tapir lives in Central America and parts of Mexico. It is the biggest wild land animal in all of Central America. This big tapir can weigh over 600 pounds.

Baird's tapirs are dark brown all over. Their face and chin are a bit lighter. A short, stiff **mane** stands up along the neck like a punk rocker's hair.

These tapirs stay near rivers and swamps. They are very shy and hard to find. People who live in the jungle may go their whole lives without seeing one!

# AMAZON SWIMMERS

A South American tapir can hold its breath underwater for over a minute while walking along the river bottom!

## Splash! A South American tapir plunges into a cool, wide river.

The South American tapir lives in forests across South America. This tapir is a real water lover! Rivers and ponds are like its second home.

It is a strong swimmer too. It dives to the bottom and walks on the river floor. Down there, it munches on plants that grow under the water.

Water also helps this tapir cool off on hot days. It soaks in calm ponds while fish swim right past. What a way to beat the jungle heat!

MOUNTAIN MYSTERIES
DID YOU KNOW?
Mountain tapirs can live up to 15,000 feet high, way above where most trees can grow!
20

# Huff! A woolly tapir trots through cold fog in the mountains.

The mountain tapir makes its home in the Andes of South America. It is the smallest kind of tapir, weighing about 400 pounds. It is also the hardest to find.

This tapir has thick, woolly fur. The air up in the mountains is often cold and damp. Its fuzzy coat works like a warm blanket.

Mountain tapirs live in **cloud forests** full of fog and mist. They eat tough plants and grass that other animals ignore. Very few people have ever seen one in the wild, making them true mountain mysteries.

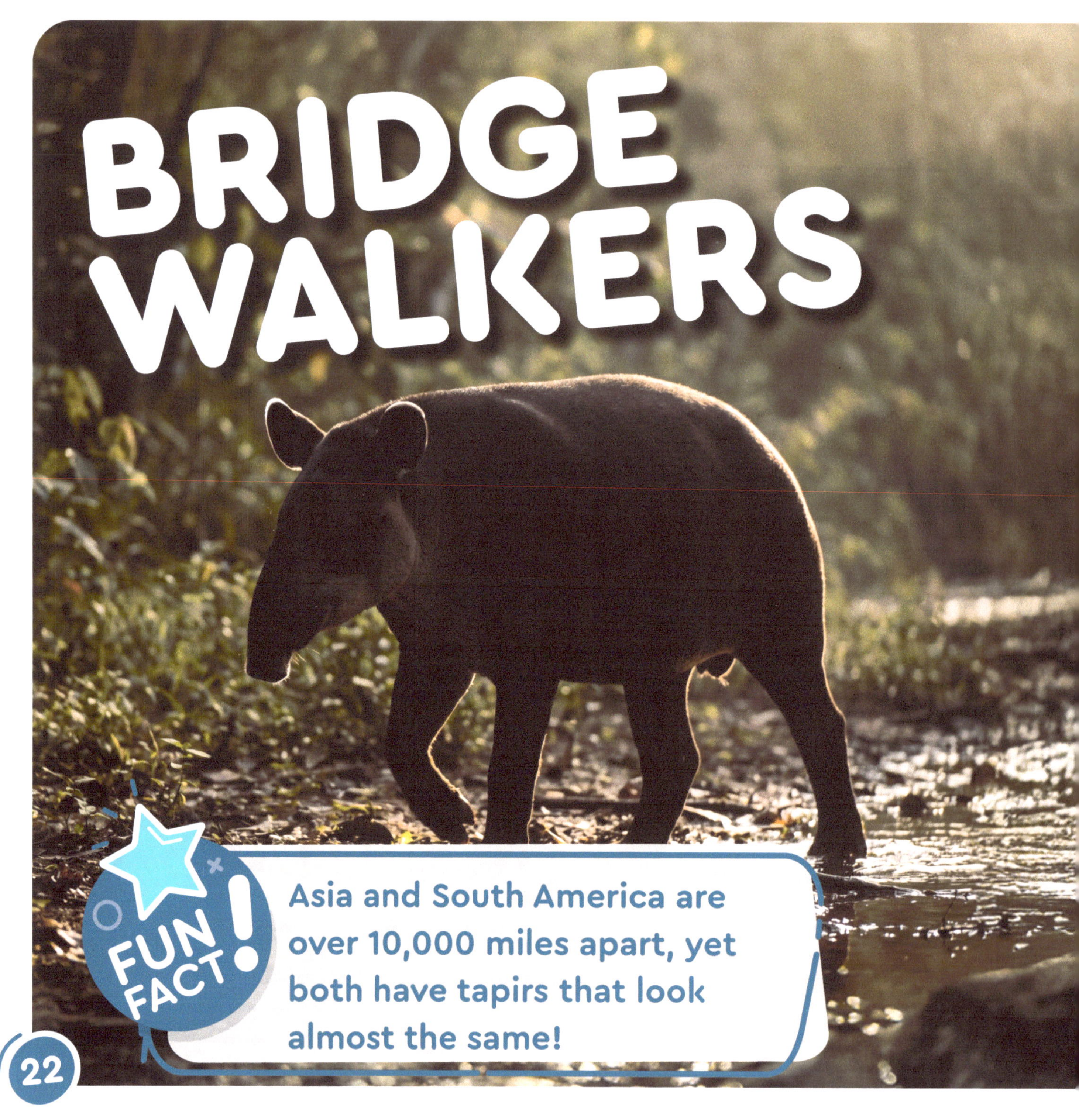

# BRIDGE WALKERS

# Tromp! Tapirs once crossed huge land bridges to reach new lands.

Tapirs live on two continents today. Three kinds live in Central and South America. One kind lives far away in Southeast Asia.

How did tapirs end up so far apart? Long ago, **land bridges** joined the continents. Tapirs walked over dry land from place to place. Then the seas rose, and the bridges went under water.

Now wide oceans keep the groups apart. But all four kinds of tapir still look much alike. That tells us tapirs once roamed much of the world together.

# TRAILBLAZERS

**DID YOU KNOW?**

Tapir paths can be over a foot deep from years of heavy footsteps, like tiny canyons in the jungle!

**Thump, thump! Heavy tapir feet stomp a path through the jungle.**

Tapirs walk the same forest paths again and again. Over time, their heavy feet press deep trails into the ground. Some people call these tapir highways.

Other animals use tapir trails too. Deer, wild pigs, and smaller critters all follow along. The tapir makes roads for the whole forest!

These trails lead to water, food, and resting spots. Tapirs know every turn by heart. They could walk their paths with their eyes closed, even on the darkest nights.

# WHISTLING WANDERERS

**Wheee! A sharp whistle rings through the dark nighttime forest.**

Tapirs come out when the forest gets dark. They cannot see very well. But their ears and nose work extra hard instead.

Tapirs talk to each other with high whistles. A mother calls her baby with a soft peep. A scared tapir lets out a loud, sharp cry that echoes through the trees.

These calls carry far through the forest. Tapirs find each other even in the darkest night. Their whistles are like a secret code only they understand!

SPLASH SURVIVAL

FUN FACT!

Tapirs will sometimes fight back, biting hard enough to break a jaguar's leg!

## Roar! A jaguar leaps, but the tapir bolts toward the river.

Tapirs have big predators to watch out for. Jaguars and pumas hunt them in the Americas. In Asia, tigers chase them through the forest.

When a tapir spots danger, it races for water. It may look slow, but a tapir can run up to 30 miles per hour! It crashes through brush and dives into the nearest river.

Once in the water, a tapir is hard to catch. It dives deep and swims to safety. Water is a tapir's best escape plan, and it works almost every time.

# SACRED SHADOWS

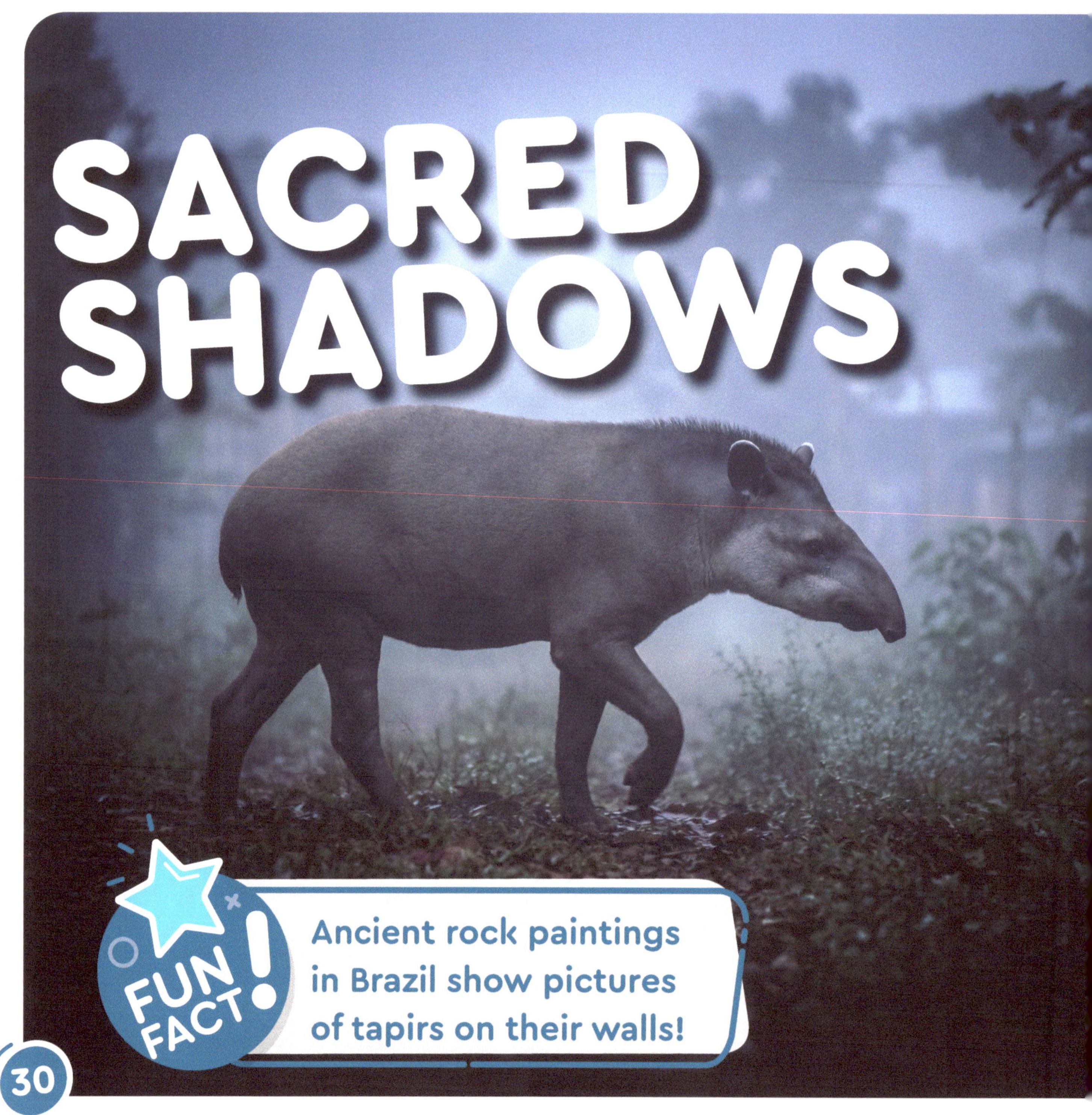

**Swish! A tapir slips past a sleeping village in the quiet night.**

People and tapirs have shared the forest for thousands of years. In South America, tapirs appear in old stories and songs. Some tales say the tapir helped shape the land itself.

In Asia, the Malayan tapir shows up in old myths too. Some stories say seeing one brings good luck. Others believe tapirs eat bad dreams!

Today, many people work to keep tapirs safe. They protect the forests where tapirs live. Tapirs may be shy, but they have many human friends around the world.

# SEED SPREADERS

**Plop! A tapir drops fruit seeds on the forest floor as it walks.**

Tapirs eat a lot of fruit. When they eat, they swallow the seeds whole. Later, seeds come out in their droppings far away from the parent tree.

This helps new plants grow all over the forest. Some people call tapirs the gardeners of the jungle. They plant trees and bushes without even trying!

Without tapirs, many plants could not spread their seeds. A single tapir can spread seeds across miles of forest. They are one of the jungle's most helpful animals.

# LOSING LAND

DID YOU KNOW?
A single tapir needs a home area as big as 500 football fields just to find enough food!

## Crack! Another tree falls as the forest shrinks all around tapirs.

All four kinds of tapir are in danger. People cut down forests to build farms and roads. This takes away the habitat where tapirs live and raise their young.

Hunting is a problem too. In some places, people still hunt tapirs for meat. Fast cars on new roads can hit tapirs at night when they cannot be seen.

The mountain tapir may be in the worst trouble. Only about 2,500 are left in the wild. If no one helps, tapirs could vanish forever after 35 million years on Earth.

# TAPIR TRACKING

People all around the world celebrate World Tapir Day on April 27, throwing parties for these amazing animals!

## Click! A hidden camera snaps a photo of a tapir at night.

Scientists are working hard to help tapirs. They hide camera traps deep in the forest. These cameras snap a photo each time an animal passes by.

The pictures show how many tapirs live in an area. Some groups put radio collars on tapirs too. The collars track where each tapir goes every single day.

People also plant new trees to bring back lost forests. New parks and safe zones protect tapir land. Every step helps keep tapirs safe for years to come.

# SPOT ONE!

The San Diego Zoo and the Nashville Zoo are two of North America's best places to see and learn about tapirs up close!

## Look! A tapir splashes through the shallow stream in its zoo habitat!

Tapirs are not easy to find in the wild. They are shy, mostly **nocturnal**, and live deep inside some of the world's most remote forests. But you do not need a plane ticket to meet one.

Many zoos across North America keep tapirs. Look for them near water — zoo tapirs love to wade and swim, and feeding time near a pool is always worth watching.

Check your zoo's website to see which species they keep. Some have Malayan tapirs, others have South American. If you spot a baby, look closely — that striped spotted coat will not last long.

# GLOSSARY

### nocturnal

Active at night and sleeping during the day

### cloud forest

A high mountain forest that is almost always covered in mist and fog

### trunk

A tapir's long, bendy nose

### land bridge

A strip of dry land that connected two continents, allowing animals to walk across

### mane

A strip of longer fur or hair running along an animal's neck or back

www.ingramcontent.com/pod-product-compliance
Lightning Source LLC
Chambersburg PA
CBHW041621110726
48005CB00002B/461